ANIMAL KINGDOM CLASSIFICATION

DWARF GECKOS, RATTLESNAKES & OTHER
REPTILES

BY DANIEL GILPIN
CONTENT ADVISER: HAROLD K. VORIS, PH.D., CURATOR AND
HEAD, DIVISION OF AMPHIBIANS AND REPTILES, FIELD MUSEUM
OF NATURAL HISTORY, CHICAGO

SCIENCE ADVISER: TERRENCE E. YOUNG JR., M.ED., M.L.S.,
JEFFERSON PARISH (LOUISIANA) PUBLIC SCHOOL SYSTEM

First published in the United States in 2006 by
Compass Point Books
3109 West 50th St., #115
Minneapolis, MN 55410

ANIMAL KINGDOM CLASSIFICATION–REPTILES
was produced by

David West Children's Books
7 Princeton Court
55 Felsham Road
London SW15 1AZ

Copyright © 2005 David West Children's Books

Designer: Rob Shone
Editors: Kate Newport, Nadia Higgins
Page Production: Les Tranby, James Mackey

Visit Compass Point Books on the Internet at
www.compasspointbooks.com
or e-mail your request to
custserv@compasspointbooks.com

Library of Congress Cataloging-in-Publication Data
Gilpin, Daniel.
  Dwarf geckos, rattlesnakes, and other reptiles /
  by Daniel Gilpin.
    p. cm. — (Animal kingdom classification)
  Includes bibliographical references (p.   ) and index.
  ISBN 0-7565-1255-7 (hard cover)
  1. Reptiles—Juvenile literature. I. Title. II. Series.
  QL644.2.G55 2005
  597.9—dc22   2005003818

PHOTO CREDITS :
Abbreviations: t-top, m-middle, b-bottom, r-right, l-left, c-center.

3, Beth Jackson, U.S. Fish and Wildlife Service; 4/5, Gordon H. Rodda, U.S. Fish and Wildlife Service; 8mt, Ray Rauch, U.S. Fish and Wildlife Service; 9t, U.S. Fish and Wildlife Service; 9mr (inset), Rosalind Cohen, NODC, NOAA; 9b, David Vogel, U.S. Fish and Wildlife Service; 12l, John Cancalosi/naturepl.com; 13b, Doug Weschler/naturepl.com; 14br, NOAA; 15m, Beth Jackson, U.S. Fish and Wildlife Service; 17t, Ingo Arndt/naturepl.com; 17m, Oxford Scientific Films; 18/18, Gary M. Stolz, U.S. Fish and Wildlife Service; 18m, Stafan Klein, iStockphoto.com; 18b, Barry Mansell/naturepl.com; 19ml, Bruce Davidson/naturepl.com; 19b, U.S. Fish and Wildlife Service; 20t, Anup Shah/naturepl.com; 20b, Jose B. Ruiz/naturepl.com; 21b, Gary M. Stolz, U.S. Fish and Wildlife Service; 22t, Mike Wilkes/naturepl.com; 22br, U.S. Fish and Wildlife Service; 23tl, Michael Pitts/natyrepl.com; 23tr, Courtesy of NPS – Canaveral National Seashore, NOAA; 24b, Courtesy of NPS – Canaveral National Seashore, NOAA; 25t, Lynn Betts, USDA/Natural Resources Conservation Service; 25m, Dennis Larson, USDA/Natural Resources Conservation Service; 28t, Mary McDonald/naturepl.com; 28b, Ed McCrea, U.S. Fish and Wildlife Service; 28/29, Acha Joaquin Gutierrez, Oxford Scientific Films; 29b, Martin Dohrn/naturepl.com; 29r, Gordon H. Rodda, U.S. Fish and Wildlife Service; 30t, Hans Christoph Kappel/naturepl.com; 31r, Jeff Rotman/naturepl.com; 31b, Anup Shah/naturepl.com; 32m, Barry Mansel/naturepl.com; 32b Oxford Scientific Films; 32/33, Paulo de Olivrira, Oxford Scientific Films; 34, Oxford Scientific Films; 34b, Neil Lucas/naturepl.com; 35tr, David Miller/naturepl.com; 35b, Beth Jackson, U.S. Fish and Wildlife Service; 36t, Peter Oxford, U.S. Fish and Wildlife Service; 36bl, Paul Guther, U.S. Fish and Wildlife Service; 36br, Tim MacMillan/John Downer Pro/naturepl.com; 38t, Gary M. Stolz, U.S. Fish and Wildlife Service; 38b, Gary M. Stolz, U.S. Fish and Wildlife Service; 39m, Gary M. Stolz, U.S. Fish and Wildlife Service; 39b, Anup Shah/naturepl.com; 40t, Florida Keys National Marine Sanctuary, NOAA; 40m, Ben Osbourn/naturepl.com; 41t, NOAA; 41b, OAR/National Undersea Research Pogram (NURP)/NOAA; 42/43, NOAA; 42b, John and Karen Hollingsworth, U.S. Fish and Wildlife Service; 43t, Robert S. Simmons, U.S. Fish and Wildlife Service; 43bl, Ryan Hagerty, U.S. Fish and Wildlife Service; 43br, David Bowman, U.S. Fish and Wildlife Service; 45b, Digital Vision.

Every effort has been made to contact copyright holders of any material reproduced in this book. Any omissions will be rectified in subsequent printings if notice is given to the publishers.

Front cover: Frilled lizard
Opposite: Desert tortoise

ANIMAL KINGDOM CLASSIFICATION

DWARF GECKOS, RATTLESNAKES & OTHER
REPTILES

Daniel Gilpin

COMPASS POINT BOOKS ✦ MINNEAPOLIS, MINNESOTA

TABLE OF CONTENTS

INTRODUCTION

Reptiles are great survivors. They flourish in deserts and other dry habitats where most other animals would quickly perish. The secret to reptiles' success is their scaly, waterproof skin. This, combined with their ability to go without food for long periods, makes them ideally suited to deserts where the air is dry and meals are few and far between.

Reptiles have the upper hand in deserts, but deserts are not the only places these tough creatures live. Reptiles can be found on every continent except Antarctica. They also inhabit many of the world's islands, often reaching new volcanic islands before any other land animals. But not all reptiles live on land. Some live in lakes and rivers, and a few even live in the ocean.

HUNTER AND HUNTED

Most reptiles are carnivores, or meat-eaters. Some lie in wait for their prey, while others actively hunt it down. This collared lizard has caught and killed a gecko, which also hunted smaller prey, such as insects.

DIVERSE AND NUMEROUS

Reptiles can be found in almost every part of the world. They exist in many shapes and forms, allowing them to survive in all sorts of different habitats. Some reptiles are bright and decorative, but most are colored for camouflage.

SUN LOVERS

Reptiles are most commonly found in the tropics. Like amphibians, they are cold-blooded. This means that they are unable to generate their own body heat and must rely on their surroundings to warm them up. When it is cold, they are cold and very inactive. Few reptiles are able to survive in places with long, icy winters. Those that do usually hibernate to avoid the worst of the weather.

Reptiles warm their bodies up by basking. As the sun rises, they creep or slither out to soak up its rays. Early morning is a dangerous time for most reptiles, as they are still too sluggish to escape fast-moving predators.

TEMPERATE
FORESTS
Copperhead snake

REPTILE TYPES

Modern reptiles fall into four different orders. The largest, Squamata, contains the lizards and snakes, with around 6,850 species. Turtles, tortoises, and terrapins also have their own order, Chelonia. It contains about 290 species, all with shells on their backs. The third largest order is Crocodilia, with 23 species. It includes the gharial and all of the world's crocodiles and alligators. Finally, there is the order Rhynchocephalia, which has just one member, the tuatara lizard.

GRASSLANDS
Texas tortoise

DESERTS
Grey-banded king snake

RIVERS AND LAKES
Alligator

JUNGLE
Chameleon

MOUNTAINS
Mountain spiny lizard

OCEANS
Green turtle

SEA LIZARDS

Most lizards keep their feet firmly on land, but one species finds its food in the sea. The marine iguana lives on the Galapagos Islands, off the west coast of South America, and feeds on seaweed. Scientists think the marine iguana evolved from a land-living species that traveled to the Galapagos aboard floating vegetation.

Marine iguana

REPTILE BODIES

All reptiles share certain physical features. Like other vertebrates, they have a bony internal skeleton with a skull to protect the brain. Some reptiles give birth to live young, but most lay eggs with tough, leathery shells. Unlike most fish and amphibians, they lay their eggs on land. Reptiles also have dry, scaly skin.

LOUNGE LIZARDS
These spiny-tailed lizards are basking in the sun. Reptiles rely on the sun to raise their body temperatures enough for them to become active. If they become too hot, they seek shade to help them cool down.

MUSCLES
Reptiles' bodies are moved by muscles under the skin. As in other vertebrates, their muscles are attached to the bones by ligaments, or tough bands of tissue.

LOOKING INSIDE
Like birds and mammals, reptiles breathe using their lungs. Even those that live in the sea must come up to the surface for air. Most reptiles have four legs and feet with clawed toes. Those without legs, such as snakes and legless lizards, evolved from ancestors that once had legs millions of years ago. The main diagram (right) shows the features of a monitor lizard, a typical reptile. Although its body shape is very different from ours, its internal organs are similar. Like us, it has a heart, liver, and complex digestive system.

Scales

SKIN AND SCALES
A reptile's skin is covered with scales made of keratin—the same substance that is in our fingernails. The scales retain water, helping reptiles to live in very dry habitats.

Skin

Pigment cells

DIGESTIVE SYSTEM

A reptile's digestive system is very similar to a human's. Food passes down a tube called the esophagus to the stomach. From there, it travels through the intestines before waste is passed out of the cloaca.

INTERNAL SKELETON

A reptile's skeleton is made up of many bones. These provide sturdy anchor points for the organs and muscles.

BRAIN

Although the brain is relatively small, it is complex.

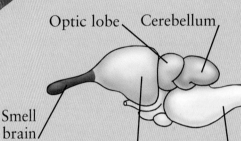

Optic lobe   Cerebellum

Smell brain

Cerebrum   Brain stem

BREATHING

All reptiles breathe air using lungs. Most reptiles have two, but some types of snakes have just one lung.

REPRODUCTION

Unlike fish and amphibian eggs, reptile eggs are fertilized inside the female's body. This and the evolution of watertight eggs are what allowed reptiles to first live on land.

THREE-CHAMBERED HEART

Blood enters the right atrium (1) and flows into the ventricle (2). From there, it is pumped to the lungs, where it picks up oxygen. It then flows into the left atrium (3) and is pumped out to the rest of the body.

1

2   3

JACOBSON'S ORGAN

Jacobson's organ helps snakes and some lizards find prey by "tasting" the air. The reptiles flick out their forked tongues to pick up tiny particles from other animals. These are detected when the tongue is drawn back in, and its tips are pushed into the organ.

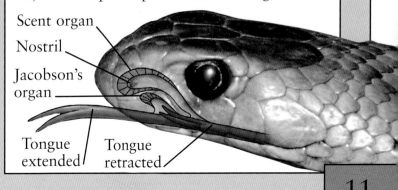

Scent organ

Nostril

Jacobson's organ

Tongue extended   Tongue retracted

11

Most reptiles today are small, but millions of years ago, reptiles were the largest creatures on Earth. The most famous giant reptiles of all were the dinosaurs.

PREHISTORIC GIANTS

Although they became extinct 65 million years ago, dinosaurs were more advanced than most reptiles today. Scientists think that dinosaurs were warm-blooded, which meant that they could be active in cold climates. Unlike modern reptiles, some plant-eating dinosaurs were able to chew their food, and many meat-eaters were probably quite intelligent. The largest dinosaurs were more than 100 feet (30.5 meters) long and may have weighed as much as 110 tons (99 metric tons).

MEGAZOSTRODON

This little creature was one of the earliest mammals. It evolved from reptile ancestors about 230 million years ago. This was about the same time as the first dinosaurs appeared.

FLYING REPTILES

Pterosaurs, such as these Pteranodon, *were flying creatures that evolved from the same reptiles as dinosaurs. Some pterosaurs were gigantic. The largest had wingspans of 37 feet (11 m).*

SEA MONSTERS

While dinosaurs roamed the land, giant reptiles swam in the seas. Long-necked plesiosaurs and speedy ichthyosaurs hunted fish. They were in turn hunted by huge pliosaurs, such as *Liopleurodon.* Most giant sea reptiles died out at the same time as the dinosaurs, but one group, the turtles, lived on.

LIVING FOSSILS

Tuataras have hardly changed since the Age of Dinosaurs. Their relatives died out 100 million years ago, but they miraculously lived on. Although the two species of tuatara look like lizards, they are classified in their own order. Unlike other reptiles, their teeth are fused to their jaws. They also have a primitive, light-sensing organ between their eyes.

Tuataras live on small islands off New Zealand.

DINOSAURS

Fossils suggest that many dinosaurs lived in groups. Plant-eaters, such as these Hypsilophodon, *formed herds for protection. Some meat-eaters, such as* Deinonychus *(above), may have hunted in packs.*

13

SKIN, SCALES, AND CLAWS

All reptiles have skin that is covered by scales. In some species, the scales overlap like armor. In others, the scales rub up against one another.

SCALES FOR PROTECTION

A reptile's scales protect its body and keep it from drying out. Reptiles that kill and eat large animals, such as crocodiles, have tough, thick scales to guard against the kicks and blows of struggling prey. Turtles and tortoises have taken the protecting role of their scales one step further. Their bony shells have evolved so that they are covered with very large, interlocking scales made of horn. These grow as the animal grows.

BELLY DANCING

Snakes use the scales on their bellies to move. They do this by contracting the skin between some scales and expanding it between others.

WATERPROOF COATS

Scales have allowed reptiles to become land animals. The dry, shiny surface of the scales forms a barrier between the animal and the air. This prevents valuable water in the body from evaporating.

SLOUGHING

Snakes and lizards literally grow out of their skins. When the reptile becomes too big for its skin, it sheds it in one piece—a process known as sloughing (pronounced "sluffing"). Most snakes and lizards slough many times.

AMAZING FEET

Geckos can stick to almost anything. Some are even able to run across ceilings or climb up glass. They can do this because the soles of their feet are covered in hundreds of microscopic claws.

Lizard's claws can act like running spikes. This zebra-tailed lizard has hooked claws at the ends of its toes. This helps it escape from predators and catch fast-moving prey.

GOING PLACES

Although a reptile's scales are quite hard, the skin between them is very stretchy. This combination of toughness and flexibility works very well, offering protection without slowing the animal's movement.

Most reptiles move using their legs. Some have very long legs and are fast movers. Others, like tortoises, are much slower. This is because they have a lot of weight to carry around. Many lizards have feet that can grip well enough to climb. Some do this by grasping with their toes, while others use their claws.

RETRACTABLE LEGS

A tortoise's legs are well armored with scales. When attacked, it draws its head into its shell and pulls its legs back, leaving only the fronts of them exposed.

GETTING A GRIP

Chameleons have fingerlike toes that let their feet grip like pincers. They also have prehensile tails, which can wrap around twigs.

15

REPTILIAN SENSES

Reptiles have well developed senses, including some very unusual ones. Some reptiles can pick up body heat, while others can use their tongues to "taste" the air.

"TASTING" THE AIR
Snakes flick out their tongues to gather particles from other animals. The fork at the end helps them judge the direction of their prey. If more particles hit the right fork, the snake turns in that direction.

EYESIGHT
Vision is the most important sense for many reptiles. Although their eyes are not quite as complex as those of mammals, reptiles see the world similar to the way we see it. Like us, reptiles see in color, although the range of colors they see is not as wide. Their eyes also work in a similar way, using flexible lenses. To focus on nearby objects, the lens is compressed, making it thicker. To focus on faraway things, it stretches and becomes thinner.

THE THIRD EYELID
A crocodile has a third, clear eyelid called the nictitating membrane. This protects the eye underwater while still allowing the animal to see.

BLIND SNAKES

Close relatives of boas, blind snakes are harmless creatures that feed on worms and insects. They hunt their prey under dead leaves, where vision is useless. So as they evolved, they completely lost their sight. Blind snakes are found in many parts of the world, including North America, but they are rarely seen because of their lifestyle.

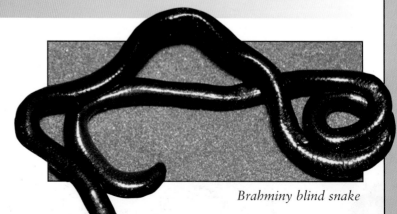

Brahminy blind snake

REVOLVING EYES

A chameleon can move both its eyes independently. When it spots prey, each eye turns toward it. This gives the chameleon binocular vision, allowing it to judge the distance between itself and its prey before firing its tongue.

Jackson's chameleon

OTHER SENSES

For most snakes and monitor lizards, the sense of taste is even more important than sight. These meat-eaters gather particles from the air with their tongues to detect prey or dead animals that are hidden or out of sight. The least-developed sense in most reptiles is hearing.

HEAT SEEKERS

Pit vipers, such as the copperhead, have special organs that detect the body heat of other animals. The organs, located on both sides of the head between the eyes and nostrils, let the snakes hunt in the dark.

ALLIGATOR LIZARD

Though ears look like simple holes, they are complex structures and are particularly good at detecting low sounds traveling through soil.

NO EARS

Snakes and some lizards have no earholes at all. This southwestern earless lizard (right) relies on its sharp eyesight to find food and stay safe.

COLORS AND CAMOUFLAGE

Reptiles include some of the most beautifully patterned and colorful creatures on the planet. Most reptiles use color for either camouflage or communication. A few use it to frighten away other animals.

BRIGHT CAMOUFLAGE

Although it looks bright, the emerald tree boa is actually colored to blend in. This South American snake spends its life in the leafy canopies of tropical trees, where it lies in wait for birds and other prey.

LOST IN LEAVES

Like the emerald tree boa, the gaboon viper is an ambush predator, but it hunts on the ground. It can lie in wait for weeks before getting the chance to strike at its prey.

OUT OF SIGHT

Most reptiles use camouflage of one kind or another. Blending in with the background helps many species avoid the attention of predators. Hiding is much safer and more energy efficient than running away. Other reptiles use camouflage to help them catch prey. Many snakes, for example, lie in wait for their victims, staying hidden until prey wanders into striking range.

The North American horned lizard combines its flattened body with sand-colored skin to make it harder for predators to see. If spotted, it sprays its attackers with blood from its eye sockets.

PARSON'S CHAMELEON

Chameleons are famous for their ability to change color for camouflage. They also have flat bodies that they sway from side to side like leaves to fool potential prey.

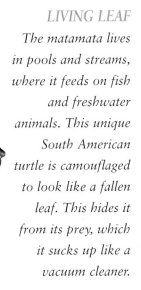

IN PLAIN VIEW

Some reptiles use color to send messages to each other. Male anole lizards, for example, have flaps of brightly colored skin beneath their chins that they open like flags to attract females. Visual signals are important to reptiles since they cannot produce many sounds. Chameleons sometimes change color to express moods such as aggression.

LIVING LEAF

The matamata lives in pools and streams, where it feeds on fish and freshwater animals. This unique South American turtle is camouflaged to look like a fallen leaf. This hides it from its prey, which it sucks up like a vacuum cleaner.

MIMICS

Some snakes use bright colors and bold patterns to warn other animals that they are dangerous. In some places, harmless snakes have evolved similar markings to disguise themselves as dangerous species. A good example of this can be seen in North America, where the harmless milk snake mimics the poisonous coral snake.

A coral snake and its harmless milk snake mimic (inset)

ON THE HUNT

Most reptiles are carnivores, which hunt live prey. Many feed on small creatures such as insects, but some kill and eat creatures as large as buffalo. Not all reptiles are hunters. A few eat dead animals, and some eat plants.

STALKING PREY

Many carnivorous reptiles hunt by stealth, creeping up on prey then striking suddenly. Some use camouflage to help them get close. Others hunt under the cover of darkness or creep up on land prey while still underwater. Despite the fact that they are cold-blooded, reptiles can move very quickly when attacking. By using the element of surprise, the reptiles increase their chances of catching their prey.

SURPRISE!
Nile crocodiles attack animals that come to the water to drink. The crocodiles detect their prey through sound and pressure waves in the water. They move slowly toward the victim before bursting out to catch it.

A STICKY END
Chameleons are slow-moving lizards. They do not need to be quick to catch prey. Instead, the lizard creeps up and shoots prey with a long, sticky tongue. The tongue itself moves quickly— almost too quick to see.

All snakes are predators. Some disable or kill their prey using venom. Others, such as this corn snake (above, above right, and main), literally squeeze the life out of prey, wrapping themselves around it so it cannot breathe. Snakes can disconnect their jaws and have very stretchy skin. This allows them to swallow prey with bodies much wider than their own.

AMBUSH

The best way to catch prey by surprise is to not move at all. Some reptiles wait for their food to come to them, staying hidden until the very last moment. The gaboon viper is one creature that hunts in this way. The disadvantage of this type of ambush hunting is that they may have to wait a long time between meals. However, unlike stalking prey, it uses up almost no energy.

FISHING WITH A WORM

Most ambush hunters wait for their prey to wander or swim toward them by chance. The alligator snapping turtle, on the other hand, actually lures its prey into its mouth. The turtle's long, round tongue looks like a worm. The turtle just lies still and wriggles its tongue to draw fish toward it.

Alligator snapping turtle

MATING, EGGS, AND YOUNG

Most reptiles reproduce by laying eggs. Some build nests then leave the eggs to develop on their own. Others stand guard over them until they hatch. A few reptiles give birth to live babies.

KEEPING GUARD

The grass snake watches over her eggs. Some snakes lay their eggs in warm spots, such as compost heaps, to help them develop. Pythons incubate their eggs, or keep them warm with their own bodies by twitching to generate heat.

FEW SURVIVORS

The majority of reptiles lay lots of eggs. Unlike birds, most leave their eggs after they lay them, which means most reptile hatchlings are in the dangerous position of having to fend for themselves. Having many babies ensures that at least a few will survive until adulthood.

LIVE BIRTHS

Some snakes and lizards are viviparous. This means that instead of laying eggs, they give birth to live young. Many viviparous species live in cold places, where it is rarely warm enough for eggs to develop. The British adder and the common lizard are both viviparous, as is the spiny lizard found in the mountains of North America.

FIGHTING RATTLERS

To win mates, male rattlesnakes perform a combat dance. They try to force each other to the ground. The winner wins the right to mate with a nearby female.

Spiny lizard

BREAKING FREE

This baby monitor lizard is wriggling out of its egg. Most reptile eggs take several weeks to hatch. The temperature of crocodile and tortoise eggs affects the sex of the young. Warmer nests produce more babies of one sex than the other.

MAKING A RUN FOR IT

Sea turtles lay eggs in pits that they have dug in sandy beaches. The babies all hatch out at once and rush into the ocean. By hatching and running together, overwhelm predators. Most of them make it to the water.

BREEDING COLORS

Male anole lizards attract mates by opening flaglike flaps of skin under their necks. Different species have flaps of different colors and shapes.

SELF-SUFFICIENT

Baby reptiles look like tiny versions of their parents. Although they grow much bigger as they become older, they hardly change shape at all. Hatchlings can run or slither right away and instinctively know how to find food. Although most die young, those that do survive can live to a great age. Crocodiles and tortoises can live to be well over 100.

FEMALES ONLY

Most reptiles have to mate to produce young but not the Californian whiptail lizard. This unusual species is made up entirely of females. The lizards lay unfertilized eggs, which hatch out as perfect clones, or copies, of their mother. This sort of reproduction is known as parthenogenesis.

Californian whiptail lizard

TURTLES AND TORTOISES

Turtles are the only reptiles that have shells, and tortoises are turtles that live only on land. Both evolved during the Age of Dinosaurs.

EGYPTIAN TORTOISE
Tortoises live in warm parts of the world, and the Egyptian tortoise is no exception. Like other tortoises, this species spends its whole life on land and feeds exclusively on plant matter.

GALAPAGOS GIANT TORTOISE
These huge reptiles can weigh 770 pounds (346.5 kilograms). The world's oldest known animal is a Galapagos giant tortoise called Harriet. She lives in a zoo in Australia and turned 175 years old in 2005.

EARLY BEGINNINGS
The first turtles and tortoises evolved around 200 million years ago, not long after the first dinosaurs appeared. Since then, they have changed little in shape and body structure. Though their design may look strange, it is very well suited to the challenges of surviving on Earth.

LEATHERBACK TURTLES

The leatherback turtle is larger than any other turtle or tortoise. Full-grown adults can be 9.5 feet (2.9 m) long and weigh almost a ton. The leatherback turtle lives in the warm and temperate waters of the open ocean where it feeds mainly on jellyfish. Like other turtles, it has to come ashore to lay its eggs. But unlike them, its shell is made up of small bony plates embedded directly in the skin.

PHYSICAL CHARACTERISTICS

All turtles and tortoises have a protective carapace, or shell. In most species, this is formed from bones covered with hornlike material. The shell is so strong that very few creatures can puncture it. It provides good protection against their natural predators, allowing turtles and tortoises to live long lives. Turtles and tortoises do not have teeth and feed using a sharp-edged beak.

CHANGING DIET

Another freshwater, North American species is the red-eared turtle. It starts life as a carnivore but turns to eating plants as it grows older.

PAINTED TURTLE

This species lives in ponds, lakes, and streams across North America. It spends the morning basking on rocks or floating logs before returning to the water to feed.

HAWKSBILL TURTLE

The hawksbill is one of just seven living species of sea turtles. It is unique because the scales on its shell overlap rather than just rub together. Female hawksbills lay larger clutches, or groups of eggs, than any other reptile—up to 242 at a time.

LIZARDS GALORE

Lizards are the most common and widespread of all land reptiles. They live on every continent except Antarctica. Lizards range in size from the minute to the monstrous. Most are meat-eaters, but a few feed on plants.

GILA MONSTER
This North American desert reptile is one of just two venomous lizards. The other is the beaded lizard from Mexico. Both Gila monsters and beaded lizards have thick tails, which they use to store fat.

DWARFS AND GIANTS
The world's smallest reptile is the Jaragua dwarf gecko, which measures just 0.7 inches (1.8 centimeters) long. It is so small that it was not discovered until 2001. The biggest lizard is the Komodo dragon.

NATURAL SURVIVORS
More than half of all the world's reptiles are lizards, with more than 3,500 known species. Lizards live in almost every habitat, from baking deserts to tropical rain forests. They are even found on islands far out at sea. Lizards can go for long periods without food or water. This allows them to survive where other creatures cannot.

KOMODO DRAGON
Komodo dragons are named after the island where they live in Indonesia. These gigantic reptiles are the largest members of the group known as monitor lizards. They can grow to 10 feet (3 m) long and can tackle almost any prey.

Australia's frilled lizard has its own unique way of scaring attackers. It flips open its neck frill and hisses to make itself seem much more dangerous.

DESERT IGUANA
Iguanas are herbivorous lizards. There are more than 700 species altogether. Most live in South and Central America.

LIVING DANGEROUSLY

Lizards have evolved special ways of defending themselves from predators. One of their most common defense mechanisms is tail shedding. When attacked, the lizard's tail falls off and twitches to distract the predator, while the lizard escapes. In most cases, the tail slowly grows back.

BASILISK

When startled, this South American lizard can rear up on its back legs and scurry away. It can even run for a few feet on water. This has earned the lizard the nickname "Jesus Christ lizard," because of the Bible story in which Christ walks on water.

LEGLESS LIZARDS

Through evolution, some lizards have lost their legs completely. This is usually an adaptation to burrowing—many legless lizards live in sandy deserts or feed on underground prey. Legless glass lizards seem to shatter when attacked. The lizard sheds its tail, which often breaks into pieces.

Glass lizard

27

SLITHERING SNAKES

HOOD UP

A cobra shows aggression by raising the hood on its neck. Cobras are highly venomous, and most animals recognize this signal.

Snakes are the ultimate reptilian land predators. Some hunt by stealth and others by ambush, but all are efficient killers. Snakes are related to lizards. Unlike their relatives, however, snakes have poor vision and rely more on taste and smell.

COLD-BLOODED KILLERS

Snakes kill their prey in one of two ways. Some, such as boas and pythons, kill by constriction. They wrap themselves around prey and tighten their coils every time it breathes, so that it is slowly strangled. Other snakes, such as vipers, use venom to kill their victims. If provoked, most snakes will bite in defense. Some have venom that is strong enough to kill humans.

PLAYING POSSOM

Hognose snakes defend themselves by pretending to die. Most predators prefer prey that looks healthy and avoid animals that look ill or dead. Hognose snakes live across most of North America.

This hognose snake is playing dead.

GABOON VIPER

This predator from the African rain forests has the longest fangs of any snake—up to 2 inches (5 cm) long. The fangs work like needles to inject venom deep into prey.

GREEN ANACONDA

This enormous boa from South America is the world's largest snake. It can grow to almost 11 yards (10 m) long and weighs more than three adult men.

BIG MEALS

Snakes have flexible jaws that they can unhinge to wrap their mouths around prey. This unique ability lets them swallow large animals. Some pythons have even been known to eat human beings.

Snakes do not chew their prey; they swallow it whole. After eating, their bodies are often so stretched out by their meal that they are almost unable to move. Some snakes can survive for months without having to feed again.

Most snakes live in warm parts of the world. Around 2,300 species have been discovered so far.

DUNENT'S BOA

Boas are large snakes that suffocate their prey. Most live in South or Central America. Boas look similar to pythons, and the two are closely related. Pythons, however, live in Africa and Asia.

BROWN TREE SNAKE

Many snakes are good climbers, and some spend most of their lives in trees. The brown tree snake lives in Guam, as well as in Australia and nearby countries.

SNAKES ALIVE!

Garter snakes live farther north than any other snake in North America. Some live within a few hundred miles of the Arctic Circle. Garter snakes survive the winter by gathering together in sheltered hideaways. They also gather in huge numbers to mate, the small males wriggling over each other as they seek out larger females.

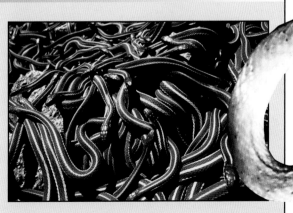

Garter snakes gather to breed.

CROCS AND GATORS

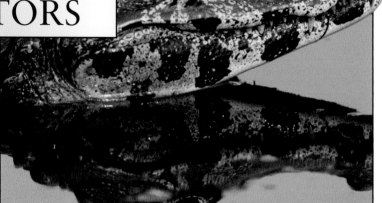

Crocodilians are some of the largest of all reptiles. There are 23 species, found in warm countries around the world.

BUILT TO EAT MEAT

Crocodiles and alligators are among the most fearsome-looking of all meat-eating animals. Their huge jaws are filled with large teeth, designed to grip and rip chunks off their prey. Crocodiles and alligators kill large animals by drowning them. They pull their victims under the water then roll them over and over until they are dead. Unlike snakes, they are not fussy eaters and will eat dead, rotting animals as well as fresh prey.

SPECTACLED CAIMAN

Caimans are small crocodilians that live in Central and South America. The spectacled caiman is the most common of the five species.

CROC OR GATOR?

A crocodile has a pointed snout (below) and teeth that are visible from the upper and lower jaws when the mouth is closed. An alligator's snout (inset) is much more rounded. When the mouth is shut, only teeth from the top jaw can be seen.

This species is almost extinct in the wild but has bred well in captivity. It may be released back into nature in parts of China. The Chinese alligator is one of the smaller crocodilians, growing to just 7 feet (2 m) long. Its main prey is fish and other river creatures, but it will attack almost any animal that enters the water.

GOING PLACES

Crocodiles and alligators are excellent swimmers, driving themselves through the water with their muscular, flattened tails. They use their legs for moving at very slow speeds and for steering.

Crocodiles don't move as well on land, but they can still get around surprisingly fast. Some species can reach 12.5 miles (20 kilometers) per hour. As they gallop along, they sometimes have all four feet off the ground at once.

WALKING TALL

Crocodiles and alligators, such as this mugger crocodile from India, walk with their legs sticking out from the sides. For short distances, they don't bother getting up. They slide along on their bellies, pushing with their legs.

SALTWATER CROCODILE

This is the world's largest reptile, reaching 7.5 yards (6.8 m) long and weighing more than a ton. The saltwater crocodile lives in rivers and coastlines around the eastern half of the Indian Ocean.

WORM LIZARDS

Few people are aware that worm lizards exist. These strange little creatures live hidden lives, burrowing through the soil in search of earthworms and insects. Worm lizards are found throughout the world but are most common in warm climates. Around 130 species have been discovered so far.

LIFE WITHOUT LEGS

Most species of worm lizards have no legs at all. In fact, they have evolved so perfectly for an underground lifestyle that they have started to resemble the earthworms they feed on. Most worm lizards are about 1 foot (30 cm) long. They belong to the same order as snakes and lizards. Unlike these relatives, however, worm lizards' bodies are surrounded by bands of scales.

OUT OF ITS ELEMENT

All worm lizards have smooth bodies, and most have very rounded heads. Above ground, they don't move easily and are easy prey for meat-eating animals. Underground, however, they have no real predators and are rarely attacked.

AJOLOTE

This Mexican worm lizard (above) uses its short front legs to help it tunnel. The feet each have five long, hooked claws for scraping away soil.

SCALY FACE

Some worm lizards look more reptilian than others. This species not only has front legs but also a very lizardlike head.

UNDER GROUND

Worm lizards, such as this European species (left), live their lives out of sight from humans. In this way, they are like reptilian moles.

TUNNEL DWELLERS

The worm lizard family has the Latin name Amphisbaenidae. This name is quite appropriate as it literally means "going both ways." The head and tail ends of a worm lizard look extremely similar, and these creatures can move through their tunnels backward as easily as forward.

Worm lizards hardly ever come to the surface but may be seen after heavy rain, when their tunnels become flooded. Although they live in darkness, they have tiny, simple eyes. The eyes are useless for finding food, so the reptiles locate their prey entirely by smell and touch.

HEADS FOR DIGGING

Worm lizards live in loose soil and dig their tunnels head first. Their skulls are specially adapted for digging and shaped to push soil apart. Some worm lizards have "keel heads." Seen from above, their skulls look like wedges. Others have skulls that are shaped more like shovels for pushing soil up and over the body.

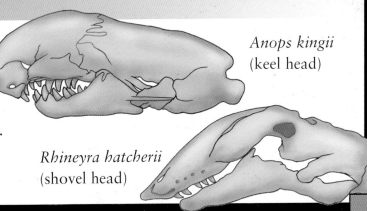

Anops kingii
(keel head)

Rhineyra hatcherii
(shovel head)

REPTILES ON DRY LAND

Reptiles are more successful in deserts than any other vertebrates. Their ability to go without water for long periods makes them ideally suited to dry habitats. Many desert reptiles do not drink at all but get all the water they need from their food.

DESERT MASTERS

Many snakes and lizards have made deserts their only home. Here, being cold-blooded is actually an advantage. They are never short of sunshine for basking in and, unlike warm-blooded birds and mammals, the reptiles don't need to use up energy keeping their bodies warm.

CHUCKWALLA

This North American lizard feeds during the day on desert plants. If threatened by a predator, it runs for the nearest rocky crevice. It then swallows air to inflate its body and wedge itself in.

SIDEWINDER

Moving over hot sand is difficult for creatures without legs. North America's sidewinder has evolved an ingenious solution to this problem. It moves by creating S shapes with its body so that only two or three points touch the sand at a time. This sidewinding movement has separately evolved in another species, too—the unrelated African viper.

FRINGE-TOED LIZARD

The long, scale-fringed toes of this North American desert lizard help it run quickly over the sand and tunnel out of danger.

MOLOCH

This Australian desert lizard is covered with defensive spikes, which give rise to its other name—thorny devil. The moloch feeds almost entirely on ants, which it laps up from the ground with its tongue.

RATTLER

Rattlesnakes are common in North America's deserts. The sound of the rattle tells other animals to keep away.

SECRETS OF SUCCESS

Another advantage reptiles have in deserts is their simple life cycle. Unlike amphibians, they do not need water to breed since they lay dry-shelled eggs. Also, their young are able to fend for themselves. That means the parents don't waste energy bringing them food or looking after them.

Reptiles are so successful in deserts that more species live there than in almost any other habitat. The main reason for this is the lack of competition. Most birds and mammals that might otherwise hunt small desert creatures are simply unable to survive without reliable sources of water.

WATER CARRIER

The Sonoran desert tortoise carries its own water supply. It drinks as much as it can after a rainfall and holds up to a pint (0.5 liters) of water in its body.

FOREST REPTILES

Forests offer many opportunities to reptiles such as snakes and lizards, many of which are excellent climbers. Tropical forests in particular are good habitats for reptiles. They provide the constant warmth and abundance of food that these creatures need.

ABOVE IT ALL

Most forest reptiles are adapted for life in the trees. Lizards either have sharp, hooked claws or special feet for gripping. Geckos, for example, can stick to tree trunks, while chameleons have fingerlike toes for grasping. Tree-climbing snakes have extremely flexible bodies. Some are muscular for wrapping around branches, while others are slender and lightweight enough to balance on tiny twigs.

TREE BOA

Adult emerald tree boas are green, as their name would suggest, but their young are red. Tree boas wrap around branches and wait for prey, which ranges from small mammals and birds to lizards.

WALK IN THE WOODS

Tortoises eat plants that grow on the ground and so are uncommon in forests. This Galapagos giant tortoise has wandered into a clearing in the woods to feed on small saplings.

FOREST FOOD

Most forest reptiles hunt other animals. A few, however, are herbivores. The forests of South and Central America have many iguanas, large lizards that climb through the trees to find the tastiest leaves.

ANOLE

Many forest lizards are green to help them blend in with the leaves. Most, such as this South American anole, are small and feed on insects that live up in the branches.

VINE SNAKE

Unlike tree boas, which lie in wait, the brown vine snake moves to find its prey. Good camouflage combined with slow, careful movements let it slither unnoticed into striking distance.

"FLYING" LIZARD

Many creatures must come down to the ground to get from tree to tree, but not the so-called flying lizard of Southeast Asia (left). It leaps into the air and opens winglike flaps of skin to glide between trees. The lizard's "wings" are supported by extended rib bones. It also uses this technique to escape predators.

FOREST FLOOR REPTILES

Most forests floors are covered with dead leaves. Reptiles here are either small enough to live under the leaves or camouflaged to look like them. The gaboon viper, which may reach 7 feet (2 m) long, is well-camouflaged and feeds on small mammals.

RIVER AND SWAMP REPTILES

Some reptiles spend most of their lives in swamps, lakes, or rivers. Two groups in particular are adapted to live in these wet habitats—crocodilians and freshwater turtles.

TRUE WATER DWELLERS

Freshwater turtles spend almost as much time in water as sea turtles. Like them, freshwater turtles have to come onto land to lay their eggs. Otherwise, they mostly stay in water. These turtles can be found in most of the world's tropical countries, but a few species live in temperate regions. The painted turtle, for example, can be found as far north as Canada.

Crocodiles and their relatives also spend most of their time in the water. Like freshwater turtles, however, most come out in the morning to bask in the sun.

WARMING UP

Freshwater turtles bask in the sun to warm up. Whenever possible, they choose rocks, branches, or sandbars surrounded by water. These allow them to quickly slide back in when danger threatens.

SNORKEL NOSE

Some turtles, such as this Texas spiny softshell, have long noses, which they poke up through the water to breathe. This helps them avoid predators above the surface. Softshell turtle shells are mostly just thickened skin.

FISH-EATER

North America's garter snakes change their diets according to what food is available. In some habitats, fish are high on their menu. They also hunt frogs and invertebrates.

LONG-NECKED TERRAPIN

This freshwater turtle hides on the bottom in shallow water and waits for prey to come toward it. Its long neck allows it to reach up and take a breath without moving its body. This way, it doesn't stir up mud and give away its hiding place.

REGULAR WATER VISITORS

Some land reptiles enter the water to hunt. In Europe, the grass snake often enters ponds to search for amphibians. Some larger snakes use water as a place to hide. Anacondas, for instance, frequent swamps, where they hunt everything from deer and rodents to other reptiles, such as caimans.

A few snakes, like the wart snakes of Australia and Southeast Asia, specialize in hunting fish. They spend so much time in the water that they actually have difficulty moving around on land.

NILE MONITOR

Despite its name, this large, meat-eating lizard lives by rivers throughout Africa, not just the Nile. It hunts both on land and in water and is an excellent swimmer and diver.

THE GAVIAL

This crocodilian specializes in hunting fish. Its long, slender jaws are filled with needle-sharp teeth, perfect for grasping its slippery prey. Gavials live in the rivers of Bangladesh, India, Nepal, and Pakistan. Their back feet are fully webbed to help them make tight turns underwater.

REPTILES AT SEA

Oceans might not seem the place for dry-skinned, air-breathing reptiles, but a number of species live in them. Sea turtles spend most of their lives in the ocean, and some sea snakes never leave it.

BEFORE DINOSAURS

There have been turtles in the oceans for millions of years. These creatures first appeared before most dinosaurs and shared the seas with other reptiles that are now extinct. Some prehistoric turtles were true giants. One, *archelon*, grew to 5 yards (4.6 m) long.

TURTLES TODAY

Although modern turtles are smaller than some of their ancestors, they can still be very big. The largest, the leatherback, can weigh almost a ton, making it one of the heaviest living reptiles. Turtles are well adapted to life in the sea, with streamlined bodies and powerful flippers.

MARINE IGUANAS

These large lizards live on the Galapagos Islands in the Pacific Ocean. Marine iguanas feed on seaweed that grows on the rocks. Adult males sometimes dive several yards below the surface to reach it.

OCEAN VOYAGER

The saltwater crocodile can make long journeys at sea to reach distant islands. It is the world's most dangerous reptile, perhaps killing hundreds of people every year.

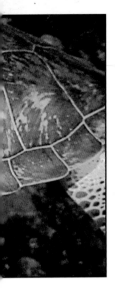

BACK TO HER BIRTHPLACE

Like all female sea turtles, the green turtle (left) returns to the beach where she hatched to lay her own eggs. At certain times of the year, individual turtles migrate from their feeding grounds to reach these beaches, with many females arriving at once.

SEA AND SAND

Some reptiles, such as the saltwater crocodile, find food in the sea but bask on land. The saltwater also lays eggs on land. It builds nest mounds of sand and vegetation, which it guards fiercely. When the eggs hatch, the mother carries the young to the water in her mouth.

LOGGERHEAD

This turtle gets it name from its unusually large head. It feeds mainly on crabs and other shellfish, cracking them open with its powerful jaws.

SEA SNAKES

There are about 60 species of true sea snakes, all related to the land-living cobras. Most sea snakes feed on fish and have the most powerful venom of any reptile. They swim with the help of flattened tails, and their nostrils have special valves for keeping out water. True sea snakes give birth to live young and spend their whole lives in the water.

Olive sea snake

REPTILES IN DANGER

Reptiles are faced with many threats, but most of their problems are caused by humans. Reptiles are hunted for food and the pet trade, and many are killed accidentally. The greatest threat to most reptiles is habitat loss.

PROTECTED
Around 8,160 reptile species are known to exist. More than 300 of these, or about one out of every 25, are threatened with extinction. Although most reptiles are safe, those that are not need protection if they are to survive. Fortunately, organizations exist to help these threatened species. A few are government bodies, but most are charities that rely on the public for funds.

REPTILE CONTRABAND
Reptiles make popular pets, but many are caught illegally from the wild. These iguanas were being smuggled when they were taken back by officials.

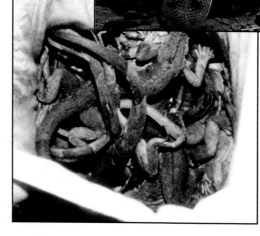

NOWHERE TO CALL HOME
As their habitats are ruined, reptiles such as this rhinoceros iguana are taken into captivity, where they reproduce in breeding colonies. Once the habitat is safe or has renewed itself, the new generation of reptiles is released back into the wild.

MIXED BREEDING

Interbreeding can cause two species to become one. Drainage of the salt marsh snake's habitat has forced it into contact with a close relative, and it is now being interbred out of existence.

LOST BEFORE BEING FOUND

Scientists worry that as rainforests are cut down, the reptiles that live in them will disappear, too. The biggest fear is that some species from unexplored rain forests might become extinct before they have even been discovered.

ACCIDENTAL DEATH

Turtles such as this loggerhead are sometimes trapped in nets set to catch fish. Unable to escape, the turtles drown and are not discovered until the nets are drawn in.

REPTILE CONSERVATION

The effort to save endangered species is known as conservation, and there are many projects that help endangered reptiles. Some of the rarest species are taken into captivity and looked after in the hope that they will breed. While this form of conservation often works, it is not suitable for all reptiles. Sea turtles, for instance, will not often breed in captivity. To help them, people collect their eggs so they can hatch away from predators.

Loggerhead turtle with tracking device (above); collecting Kemp's ridley sea turtle eggs (right)

ANIMAL CLASSIFICATION

The animal kingdom can be split into two main groups, vertebrates (with a backbone) and invertebrates (without a backbone). From these two main groups, scientists classify, or sort, animals further based on their shared characteristics.

The six main groupings of animals, from the most general to the most specific, are: phylum, class, order, family, genus, and species. This system was created by Carolus Linnaeus.

To see how this system works, follow the example of how human beings are classified in the vertebrate group and how earthworms are classified in the invertebrate group.

ANIMAL KINGDOM

VERTEBRATE

PHYLUM: Chordata

CLASS: Mammals

ORDER: Primates

FAMILY: Hominids

GENUS: *Homo*

SPECIES: *sapiens*

INVERTEBRATE

PHYLUM: Annelida

CLASS: Oligochaeta

ORDER: Haplotaxida

FAMILY: Lumbricidae

GENUS: *Lumbricus*

SPECIES: *terrestris*

There are more than 30 groups of phyla. The nine most common are listed below along with their common name.

Annelida (SEGMENTED WORMS)

Arthropoda (ARTHROPODS)

CHORDATA (CHORDATES)

Cnidaria (CNIDARIANS)

Echinodermata (ECHINODERMS)

Mollusca (MOLLUSKS)

Nematoda (ROUNDWORMS)

Platyhelminthes (FLATWORMS)

Porifera (SPONGES)

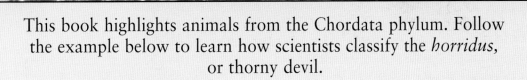

This book highlights animals from the Chordata phylum. Follow the example below to learn how scientists classify the *horridus*, or thorny devil.

VERTEBRATE

PHYLUM: Chordata

CLASS: Reptilia

ORDER: Squamata

FAMILY: Agamidae

GENUS: *Moloch*

SPECIES: *horridus*

Thorny devil
(horridus)

GLOSSARY

AMPHIBIAN
A member of the vertebrate class Amphibia; amphibians include frogs, toads and newts

BASK
To lie in the sun to warm up

BINOCULAR
Looking in the same direction with both eyes, so that the fields of vision cross over

CAMOUFLAGE
The disguising of an animal by the way it is colored and patterned to blend or merge with its surroundings

CARNIVORE
An animal that eats other creatures

CHAMELEON
A lizard with a prehensile tail, opposable toes, and skin that can change color

CLOACA
The hole on a reptile's body for getting rid of waste, as well as secreting sperm or eggs

COLD-BLOODED
Having a body temperature that varies with the temperature of an animal's surroundings, so that it is cool in cold weather and warm in hot weather

CONSTRICTION
Tightening coils to squeeze prey to death

CROCODILIAN
A member of the order Crocodilia, including crocodiles, caimans, alligators, and gavials

EVOLUTION
Change in living things through time as they become adapted to their environment

EXTINCT
Died out

FAMILY
The grouping in animal classification between order and genus

FANG
A long, pointed tooth; the fangs of some snakes are used to inject venom

GECKO
A lizard with flattened, sticky feet that let it climb up vertical surfaces

HABITAT
A particular type of environment where plants and animals live, such as a desert

HATCHLING
A baby that has just hatched from an egg

HERBIVORE
An animal that eats plants

HIBERNATE
To sleep through the winter with all body processes slowed down to save energy

LATIN
The language used by ancient Romans; scientists use it to classify animals today

MAMMAL
A warm-blooded vertebrate that feeds its young on milk and is covered with hair or fur

MIMIC
When a harmless animal resembles a harmful animal as a form of self-protection

ORDER
The grouping in animal classification between family and class

PARTHENOGENESIS
When a female animal produces young without having mated with a male

PREHENSILE
Able to grip or hold

REPRODUCTION
The process by which a new generation of animals is created

REPTILE
A cold-blooded vertebrate with dry, scaly skin; most reptiles lay eggs with watertight shells, although some give birth to live young

TEMPERATE
Having to do with areas immediately north and south of the tropical regions; temperate regions genereally have warm summers and cool winters

TROPICS
Between the Tropic of Cancer and the Tropic of Capricorn on the world map; the tropics are mostly warm and wet

VENOM
A liquid poison used to injure or kill prey

VIVIPAROUS
Able to give birth to live young

WARM-BLOODED
Able to generate heat internally to keep the body warm

FURTHER RESOURCES

AT THE LIBRARY
Hammerslough, Jane. *Snakes! Face-to-Face.* New York: Scholastic, 2003.

Jay, Lorraine. *Sea Turtles*. Minnetonka, Minn.: NorthWord Press, 2000.

McCarthy, Colin. *Reptile*. New York: Dorling Kindersley, 2000.

Townsend, John. *Incredible Reptiles*. Chicago: Raintree, 2005.

ON THE WEB
For more information on this topic, use FactHound.
1. Go to *www.facthound.com*
2. Type in this book ID: 0756512557
3. Click on the *Fetch It* button.
FactHound will find the best Web sites for you.

INDEX